Guesswork

Also by Jeffery Donaldson

Palilalia
Waterglass
Once Out of Nature

Jeffery Donaldson
GUESSWORK

Edited by Anne Compton.
Cover photograph: *88 Roxton Road, from the Threshold series by Lisa Klapstock, 2001-2002, www.lisaklapstock.com.
Cover and page design by Julie Scriver.
Printed in Canada.
10 9 8 7 6 5 4 3 2 1

Library and Archives Canada Cataloguing in Publication

Donaldson, Jeffery, 1960-
    Guesswork / Jeffery Donaldson.

Poems.
ISBN 978-0-86492-621-0

    I. Title.

PS8557.O527G84 2010   C811'.54   C2010-905315-X

Goose Lane Editions acknowledges the financial support of the Canada Council for the Arts, the Government of Canada through the Book Publishing Industry Development Program (BPIDP), and the New Brunswick Department of Wellness, Culture, and Sport for its publishing activities.

Goose Lane Editions
Suite 330, 500 Beaverbrook Court
Fredericton, New Brunswick
CANADA E3B 5X4
www.gooselane.com

For my sisters
Tracy and Lisa

Contents

Guillotine

Body and mind were never at home
under the one roof, that bare dome, high arched
by design. I often wished for a quiet loft,

a hidden vault's vertiginous lift,
where a swift whimsy's flitter and dip
might dart from any sheltered nook.

But I always found it discomfiting
how such easy drifting under the wide spans,
dusted with sunrays, could shelter in me

such squabble and cluck, unstifled
hoots and coos, unnerving sails across
a metaphoric gap's precipitous drop.

Those were early days, when the Touretter's
robotic urge was a giddy exuberance
I chose when I liked, or believed I did:

the sudden erratic rupture, the blunt nod,
awkward elbowings and verbal kicks I swore
I did for fun, any time they garnered

the inquisitive stare. I've made my peace
with the spinning dynamo's monotonous hum,
engine's run-on, clockwork's unnerving tick.

Somewhere above, a sloshed puppet master
grapples his tangled lines — the heartless jerk! —
pulling my leg. No unmangling the doublespeak,

the trickster-muse's obscure hieroglyphic,
his cryptic morse tapping itself out in broken
longs and shorts. "It's all in your head,"

the doctors claimed, for whom a tic's
"involuntary" thrust meant *having no control*,
not the nature of the compulsion driving it.

"And these worries that you're always taking on —
your home ruined by floods or abandonment,
faces you make out in the curtain pleats,

imagined footsteps on the attic boards —
aren't worth all this twisting and squint. Don't
lose your head over things you cannot change."

Somehow, the effort always brings to mind
the Humber Lodge Annual Christmas Party
and Magic Show, the redeemer's advent

rivalled by a local wizard's low-budget spoofs.
His job we knew was to kill the restless time
before the handing out of gifts. The magician

was rigged to the hilt, hoops and hats, streamers
to yank from ears red with embarrassment,
a wand for summoning illusion's fickle boon,

and for the evening's coup, grandly unveiled,
a "medieval" guillotine, it's blooded rusty blade
hung from loosely tied lines ominously frayed.

"A volunteer from the audience, please. You there,
lad in the front row, you have a good head
on your shoulders, step up!" Oh God, not me.

I was a dead man walking, unsteady legs,
head filled with gauze, all eyes fixed upon me
from a crowd braying for amazement.

"Kneel on the stool, son, your shoulders here."
He pointed to the lower board's half moon
carved to match the upper dropped on top.

I was an outlaw convicted without trial
for sticking my neck out, clamped down upon,
the offending part made to keep still.

"Good heavens, is my basket large enough
for a bean this size? Can you help me out?
Just reach around and hold your ears, like this.

That's very good! Any last words? Chin up!
You can look down…it isn't a long drop!
Now everyone count together, *One, Two*...."

Brains hung in abeyance, eyes squeezed shut,
the seconds pooled into a giddy drift,
a heady wavering stilled in vertigo.

Whatever happened next, a blank, as though
memory itself, beyond recall, had flopped
into the bucket with an awful stare, rudely

cleaved, struck by its own deliverance,
at last thinking of nothing but itself.
There must have been a clang and thunk.

The interlocking blades' precarious latch,
tripped by a falling tension and release, .
went through the motions of cutting loose.

A pending judgement had passed through me.
I was excused, pulled myself together,
light afoot, and rose to dizzying applause,

when something heavy came into my hands.
I twitched a nod and, as the tics came back,
carried my gift away and found my place.

Fetal

Unlikely twin, you and I are one.
 You are the mortified infant I outlived,
when you squirmed breathless through the mother
 of all passage rites and died looking back.

And I your still kicking representative,
 who tried, like you, his entire days
aglow with how little, to go toward the light,
 with results that don't improve with age.

The day will be, now that Palliative Care lies
 by sheer caprice one short flight above
Neo-natal, you will come to mind once more.
 You had your whole life behind you,

laid aside a heart Mother kept listening for,
 on whom it never dawned that a red womb
was all of evening skies that you would know,
 a-swim in atmospheres pinked on shut eyes.

So too, pulsing life-supports and the tossing
 bedclothes' ebbing amniotic will leave me sipping
at the intravenous bag's stingy umbilicus.
 Curtains. Familiar voices on the other side.

Will I fold up like you, feet in my hands,
 forehead to knees tucked inward
like fine origami, into what unknown form
 I wouldn't feel was in me until then?

13

It won't be as I had dreamed it, dozing off
   under the shade of an arching palm
that rises near chattering waters, tree
   filled with mourning doves' hosannas.

You faced your future early by turning in:
   not in your deathbed miming *tableau vivants*
of stormy captain on the bowsprit, grappling
   the foremast stays and craning chin up

at the plunging deep, or shoulders squared
   to meet the cosmetician *deus ex machina*,
indifferent graces, bestowed on no matter whom,
   to pretty up the nervous virgin bride.

My Ouroboros, you showed how to swallow
   losses, how to be consumed with almost
everything you leave, fill up on a vanishing
   you can never reach, full of your own hunger.

My tucked-in emptier out, always of two minds,
   my borne brother, my twin, we are not all
that we might have been when palms reached down
   to shelter us and skies were streams of bathed-in

jostling waters where we briefly dreamed. Let's go
   with wincing smiles and pass clear through
to heartbroken arms in what new world
   entirely, already loved, grieved, and still born.

Three-quarter Glosa

First, there is a mountain.
Then there is no mountain.
Then there is a mountain again.

Short-sighted toddler, as the story goes,
I stood one autumn day by a blurred lake.
The upper cloud hills rolled on the horizon,
mirrored side-angling in the still water
holding me spellbound. The surface depths
drank their reflection the way a fountain
will pour down its lathering cumulus
bubbling at the top from jets rising to it
from the inside out. I saw the image
first. "There is a mountain!"

I pointed into the water shallows:
the cloud-shine, upturned but untoppled,
echoed a kind of continental pass
that opens out in long receding peaks
with breaking mists that water down their sides.
Did I risk a journey into the vast glen,
or venture a step, and find the rock's
flawed undulant footings smashed to ripples,
as by a god's boot? Did I learn just
then there is no mountain

that can rise clear of its own likeness?
Or did an infant wisdom already know
how faith in what isn't there, eddying up
from the long daze, is more unwatered down
than firmer grounds. It shows the circling way,

and how to start on foot, the moment when —
not clouding our own visions out of mind,
the stilled reflection with a wider view
of inner lights that reach us now and
then — there is a mountain again.

Book I

The first book is made of birchbark,
on which a borer with no thought

but for nourishment insinuates
a wriggling, intermittent cuneiform.

The bark curls back, dried and peeled,
like a folded page, and thereafter

the marks become unread secrets,
a story in itself, meaningless

but for an illiterate wind that pores
over it, pausing at the pictures.

On Reading *When You Are Old*

for Annette

The number of things we have said
to each other about love is as endless
as we are. But time, if memory serves,
has written some of them down

for us and made a kind of book,
one that has no title on the cover
and lacks chapter breaks to help readers
by lamplight on solitary evenings

know where the rests fall,
where to fold a page corner or set
a bookmark to find the place
once more when they come back to it.

And to be honest, we have found
little time for reading, though we have
watched the book grow heavier
with unseparated pages thin as India paper,

and covered with words we imagined
we were still waiting for, the words
that, once we found them, we always said
we would read together in time.

It is like those nights when you dream
about writing, and your pen
flits back and forth across
the page with a scratching sound,

and the ink runs, and every least scribble
seems like a line from a poem, perhaps even,
though it is still all but obscured,
the love poem you had long planned

to write, and you look down to see
what it says and find that none
of it makes any sense because there were
no words, or only words so long

as you didn't try to read them,
and the knowledge brings you back,
and you wake in the early light
and look about you and see a book

19

on the bedside table with a bookmark
set somewhere near the beginning,
and you realize, how you couldn't say,
that you are the solitary reader.

A Note to My Poem

Listen. You and I have come a long way
since that first time we set out together
among the river clouds in the evening

and found the paper trees cool to the touch
after the sun went down, and shared a word
about them and were surprised like first-time

lovers to find ourselves, as we always joked,
on the same page. Those were days when following
the river-turns was only an excuse to get

more closely in touch with our shared feelings,
making up stories about them we knew the other
would love, racing to finish one another's sentences.

And there was that windy day when we said the river
and the trees beside it were the same as us,
that with a bittersweet longing they too had appeared

in search of purposes they thought they lacked,
and found only ourselves reaching out to them
and the breezes that were passing there anyway.

And we laughed, for the river had no eyes
to find its way, and the trees only followed along
because it was water and they were thirsty.

And as for us, I know as time went on that we grew
impatient with what the other seemed incapable
of saying, or even worse, refused to say, when it

would have solved everything just to have heard it
spoken, and we had to forgive each other
for that silence, and were never certain that we had.

Now I have used up my time and left you
alone here, repeating to yourself, not even aloud
or where any listener is likely to hear you,

the line about the river and how it looked,
the line about the trees and the indifferent breezes
that sadly in the end they had to settle for,

how there was always something in them
that we missed. But say it as often as you can,
and put in a word for me, if you think of it.

21

On the Return of Allegory

In the season of first bells, at dawn,
in the distance across the valley you can
see the embarrassed castle at last
rising clear out of the dissolving fog.

The great experiment with zero has failed.
For the king within, there was meant to be no end
to the sound of the false regalia jangling
from the upper turrets, haunting the villagers

in their beds with unnerving whistles
out of an icy wind. The flagpole lines clattered,
as from the rigging of topsails, and the sundial
threw shadows over every passing minute.

The high, long-garrisoned chambers
have grown stale from the endless winter,
and the window shutters huddle together
around the unopened, stifling magnitudes.

But now the weather has cleared a little,
and the distant villagers have come out
from their houses and approach casually
in distracted groups along the empty road.

Even now the king is saying less and less,
but the bittersweet mantra no longer dies
on his lips the way it used to. His shut eyes
do little now but show him what he cannot see.

He has left every stone he can think of unturned,
dead still at anchor on the battlements
where he takes his last look, knowing finally
that as the villagers come strolling along the roads

laughing and talking, they will feel welcomed
to a home made strangely ready for them, its emptiness
like the note left on a table by the one who,
very sad to say, could not be there when they arrive.

Book II

Lean-to. You are an improvised
shelter from winter winds.

Tweezers. You pick up
small things without breaking them.

Bellows. You breathe
when you open and close.

Pleated paper fan. There is cool
and shade in your unfolding picture.

Hinged diptych frame. Your story
is about this & that.

Cellar trap door. Lifted,
you are a way down into earth.

Skeletal jawbone. What is the word
in your empty mouth?

Ancient pyramid. Within you
are the remains of one

who lived, a few symbols scattered
around him for a journey

that most now think he was
a fool to believe in.

Torso:
Variations on a Theme by Rilke

for Wayne Rosen

Archaic Torso of Apollo

We cannot grasp his outlandish head,
where the eyes once ripened like apples.
But his Torso still shines like a candelabra
in which his look, turned back down

to a luminescence, lasts. Otherwise, the curve
of his breast couldn't blind you, nor a smile
penetrate to that midst, in the lazy furl
of his loins, where all begetting starts.

Otherwise, this stone wouldn't look put off
and small under the flow of its transparent shoulder,
wouldn't glisten like a wild animal's fur,

nor break out suddenly from its every limit
like a star. For here there is nothing
that cannot see you. You must change your life.

— *Rainer Maria Rilke, trans. J.D.*

I

His missing head is amazing. It is not for you
to know the apple of his eye, softening.   .
But the torso glows as by its own candlelight
with a gaze that, turned all the way down,

gathers and gleams. How otherwise be
dazzled by the turn of the breast, or sense
an elation permeate through the muscled loins
still deeper to where the fatherstuff burns.

How else might the hacked stone seem to rise
faceless under the dropped shoulder you can look
into, or shine like the pelt of a wild animal,

and burst out beyond itself like a dying star.
Everything you see here, chiseled and broken,
says you should make something of yourself.

II

The statue has no head. But without one
the remaining torso can see all around it
by a light that shines, it seems, from the inside,
that fills with your gaze and then gleams with it.

That's why the breast's receding ellipsis
caresses you the way it does, and why
you can't help but smile the way the groin,
with its dark secrets, looks so inviting.

That's why you get such a lift staring down
into the broken rock so badly mangled
you feel like a carnivore scavenger.

A dying star when it bursts might well see
everything at once, and from every side.
If it were a life, there would be no looking back.

III

What a rip off, this one's got no head!
Funny how they leave the damned thing out,
wrecked the way it is. And ballsy of them,
shining the lamp right where the rock is broken,

like they want you to see that you're not
really getting the full bang for your statue buck.
I wonder that more people here aren't staring,
what with the buff pecs and all, his weird package

just out there. I bet if some gay guy looked
long enough he'd get a rise out of it,
stalk it like some crazy wolf on the prowl.

Now why am I feeling that the whole room
is looking my way? Those two over there,
like I was a star or something. Or is it just me?

IV

Papa, look, here's a funny one!
How come he has no head? Do you think
someone dropped him and he broke?
Can you lift me up? I want to look down

at the neck where the break is.
Wow, he's made of rock on the inside too!
Hey, know what? His thingy
looks just like the one on the Ken doll.

Hold me steady, so I can climb up behind.
You know, like with those cardboard
movie stars at the fair where the head
is cut out, leaving a big hole in the middle

big enough to put your face into.
We'll take a picture for the Show and Tell
board at school and everyone will see me.
They'll think I'm someone else!

V

This way folks, gather around.
Thank you. With this piece, "Male Torso,"
dating from the fifth century, BCE,
critics have noted resemblances

to the statue of Apollo, sculpted
by Kanachos of Sikyon
for the temple at Didyma.
I bet you didn't know the old man

lost his head over Daphne did you?
I say I bet you didn't know....
Never mind, I'll work on that one.
Apollo as you know was the god

of truth and light, also medicine, healing,
and of course poetry and the arts.
That's what poetry is, a poet once said
to me: a figure without a head,

though I'm not sure what he meant.
I'll just lower the room light and turn
this one down like so... there,
to help draw out the sinew textures

and lively abdominal detailing, which...
Oh, Madam, we ask that our guests
not touch the stone. No, not even lightly,
and yes, even if it is already broken.

Very funny. No, not there either please.
It doesn't matter if there are fingerprints already,
that isn't the point. Even hard stone
can go soft with too much rubbing.

As I was saying, this fine specimen
of the high classical period was unearthed
in the theatre at Miletus in Asia Minor
only one hundred and fifty years ago.

Think of all that time gone by
before the poor man could see the light
of day. I like to think of his head,
even now, the open eyes still buried

somewhere below, waiting to wake up.
He's become a star attraction for us,
and I think that's because he doesn't have it,
his mind I mean. Ever wonder how

that would feel, being pure body,
a thoughtless dumb animal? Makes you think.
Next room, folks, there to the left, yes,
to the cabinet with the Grecian urns.

Ma'am, I'll have to ask that you keep up
with us. No, I'm sorry, you can't.
Look, there are surveillance cameras
up there in every corner. Lady, get a life!

VI

The head goes on last
when you dress a mannequin.
First, you have to get the lighting
right, show how the muscles

ride in their own wake just so,
before you put the clothes on.
And whatever fashions you work with,
the body has to come through

in the end, like this one, all angular chest,
the chiselled look, good six-pack,
the V-shape vector, his action
all snug and tidy inside bikini briefs.

But you don't leave it at that.
It's an art form, being a dresser,
working with the parts of things.
Most people don't even take time

to look, or appreciate, for instance,
how I've made this one suggest
a restless impatience, a breaking out,
...you know, like it didn't want

to be a mannequin any more,
wanted to come alive or change
into the one thing it wasn't. People
should empathize when they pass.

I would never tell this to the boss,
but sometimes I leave the head
on the floor just there beside the body,
its face turned to the street,

and then I hang around to see
if people notice that they are being
watched back. But I don't know,
it doesn't seem to make any difference.

VII

After a bomb explodes next to it,
and especially when the head
is taken right off the way this one is,
a body will often lie down just so

by a dusty roadside covered with mines,
or in a trench, not curled for sleep,
but as though a comedian in a charade
were "doing" someone fallen over

in shock: on his back, arms and legs
in the air, shaking. The best jokers
will keep it up long after
you've stopped thinking it funny.

They're not always this naked,
but a severe blast can tear the clothes
open so easily, you would think
he'd stumbled from an unplanned tryst,

someone in love trying to get at him
in a hurry, chest glistening with sweat
showing through where the buttons
ripped, belt and buckle flung aside

and his manly V lines under
the washboard abs guiding your eye
into the midst, the lazy, private
centre where a young man does most

of his thinking about the future.
Not this one of course, the head
being gone, and not likely to be found,
I should add, in all this muck and water,

where likely it would look like fur
off a dead animal. But sometimes,
if we're lucky, the stars come out like this,
at dusk, pretty up there in patterns

filling the sky with shining eyes all over.
You have to figure a man without a head
would be the last thing on earth
they would have imagined illuminating.

35

VIII

A body but no head. Why doesn't it look
worse off than it does? Like it didn't
need to see, still had everything a man
needs to be a man, the way a broken stone

feels lighter for being broken, like you
suddenly see things from the inside out,
the centre of a star bursting so brightly
it can blind you, if you give it some thought.

IX

All you can look at
is missing eyes. This headless
torso is too much.

X

Broken Apollo, what is it you keep
looking to say, but can't?

You are salvaged from a time when all
that escaped us was carved in stone,

when gods' bodies had heads whose mouths
were closed, or even if they spoke

used the nouns and predicates we said
we were never meant to hear.

It was your not saying what you knew
that *made* you a god,

and our not knowing what you said
that made us less than one,

and you lived by that silence,
the thought of which filled us with craving.

It must be that you haven't heard,
but we moderns have no mind for gods,

are more likely to go on about how full
of emptiness you are, how emptiness

emptied out is apocalypse. Do you feel
more human now than you did,

now that your head's memory is gone?
Like us, do you think of it somewhere

back in the old country where it lies
wide-eyed, tilted sideways in the earth?

How consoled your head must feel
dreaming of you, the one it never loved

lording it over, how you were taken up
out of the dark and rose into some kind

of heaven surely, where there is no shame
in being seen, where every broken body

is loved, stood by, and watched over,
it guesses, by curious unchanging gods.

Book III

I sniff your pages, thumb fanned,
from front to back, back to front.

I am addicted, stirring your musts,
your spine glues, your inks

and endpapers, the weak sweet
of pulp, your woody tones

like varieties of steeped tea.
If you were a madeleine out of Proust,

you would reveal a purpose
in nostalgia, memory

of a feeling long forgotten
(now faintly cured) that someone

perhaps once put in a love letter,
its pages pressed in a book.

Enter, PUCK

I Faceoff

There would be no false starts.
  Every pending poem
would open with a graceful
  wink like this, a sudden

falling into *medias res*, a pointed
  and symmetrical easing-back
into chaotic flows and the myriad
  incalculable momentums.

Moments ago, you were
  a team player, circled away
from your impasse and allowed
  another line's fresher approach

to come forward. And in the pause,
  you took stock of where
you had got to, when the thing
  you were after was lost sight of

and you found yourself pushing
  hard against your own worst enemy.
Now a light tap on the shoulder,
  you muse, is all you need

to feel summoned again, called
  to rise up and glide widely towards
the waiting one, who holds, who keeps,
  who knows when the time has come,

who lowers his hand and, not showing
   when, with a flourish drops
at your feet that single point
   you will scramble to control.

And truth be told, that's how you like it,
   since in best worlds you never know
when the good thing to play with
   will fall to you out of nowhere,

only that you agree once more
   to see what might happen
if it did. So you enter the zone,
   the inner circle, and already ready

drift imperceptibly closer
   to the zero point, hunch
over your work, and expecting nothing,
   take what is freely given.

II Defencemen

Zen artists, they look at everything backwards.
"The game isn't about getting ahead,
it's about not falling any farther behind
than we already are. The rest is out

of our hands." They see how things go,
that we always face the future in reverse,
the way Eliot said we ride on subway cars,
seated backwards, the past receding,

and god knows what lies behind us up ahead.
When the play turns, they like to give ground,
take the adversary as he comes, as a disciple might.
They prostrate themselves. They fall upon their knees.

They put themselves in the way of danger
for the greater good and are prepared
to do serious time if it means one less shot
in the world. They don't shy from people,

but prefer to see the painful give-and-take,
the alarming scrimmage, constantly
pulling away from them into the distance.
In moments of crisis they are not aloof,

work to remove obstacles and clear views.
Cowboys at heart, they can circle the wagons,
face showdowns one-on-one, grapple feisty ones
broken loose, stare down the six-shooters.

Their sticks are tools, not to carry pucks,
but to work things loose, leverage, thread,
cantilever, and divide. They go into corners
with the measured eye of a carpenter.

They have seen too many fast ones slip past,
but believe that an honest man can learn
from experience if he tries. Is it wisdom
or cowardice, that when their own side drives

headlong at sudden opportunities,
they hang back, cautious and doubtful,
certain that what they do to others, in turn
will be done to them, sooner or later?

Forwards thrive on the dicey squeak-through,
the puck-cum-billiard ball's indeterminate
calculus. Defencemen chide deflections,
and would no more live by chance than a god does.

When opponents' salvos fail — the goal unscored,
the narrow miss, the fans ablink that the team
has dodged a bad end — they drift off to their rest,
faithful that nothing happens for a reason.

III Play-by-Play

Am I a shadow of my former self, my days
spent calculating losses by the word?
Would-be action hero, I was the too-eager,
rotten defenceman, skated backwards
as though on stilts and turned like a man
digging dirt out with a shovel. At shinny
I was the town all-star, could stickhandle
and shoot, stand my ground between the pipes
staring down rock-hard frozen tennis balls
drilled by the bullies five years my senior.

I used to stay out after everyone went home,
swooping slapdash Mahovlich circles
around the goal, playing all positions,
going top corner, making phantom saves,
adding commentary and the play-by-play.
Now here's Cournoyer breaking in ... drop pass
to Beliveau, cuts on the Short S–i–i–i–i–de, Ohhh ...
how did Gamble get his glove on it!
throwing with my right hand what the left snatched
wildly from under the crossbar, pads stacked.

Or having to do it all myself, of course,
help the Leafs make one more implausible
comeback in the last minutes, down nine goals:
Under ten seconds to go! There's Keon
over the line, cutting in on the wing ...

Keon closing in, a scramble in front,
rebound... backhand... he Sco-o-o-o-res!
stick raised in the air (if no one looked),
a long deep exhalation standing in
for the sold-out Garden's ecstatic roar.

At times I would just lie on my back at dusk,
and call the play-by-plays I knew by heart —
the breathtaking rush, the drop pass, sweep check,
sound of the post clank and puck wobbling
like a thrown tire along the goal line
in the Cup final's seventh-game overtime.
And maybe it wasn't even hockey anymore,
something that spelled the hour, the March sky
drifting from itself unnoticed, like the goalie
who, when the action turns up ice, grows small.

Or maybe it was just the lines themselves
and how they handled, how they took the lead,
cut wide arcs or crossed over, backchecked,
corralled a carom, relayed or hung back,
faked inside-out, wound up and let go,
and threw everything they were spiralling
into a breathtaking wordless ether
in their ecstasy, when a light went on.
All quiet but for a child's falsetto, used
when a played-out dream life is not his own.

And what if my adult ghost were passing near,
summoned by that voice long unrecalled,
and knowing all too well the loner's mind,
and why he lay there talking in the night
when any fool could see the game was up.

Would he have listened in, heard in himself
the verbal pantomime, the impromptu
and rhapsodic counterfeit like a winter mist
rising in the clear, or pass him by instead,
knowing how it ends, and not breathe a word?

IV The Referee

In the beginning, darkness and frozen water,
above which lights plink and brighten.
The lone one circles and the space fills in.
High-strung stars drift and divide now

on both sides of the milky firmament
and slowly gather into mirrored symmetries.
Two jockey around the tempting fruit
dangled in their midst. The rest we know.

V Linesmen

Wisdom's secret is detachment not withdrawal,
   said Northrop Frye, who was not thinking
of these watchers over the lines, selfless
   students of geometrical vectors and tangents,
though he was nothing if not one himself.

   See how they are drawn to what happens,
yet steer shy of encounters when they near,
   or how, like salvagers, they keep their distance
till a stop in the game, then move in to pick up
   what others have left off caring about.

Do they see the same sport that we do? Not the play
   so much as the mechanisms and ligatures of play,
not a dash of heroes into the offensive zone,
   but the spatial relation of sticks and limbs to a black
dot passing foremost or late over a demarcation.

They watch the formations widen and converge
   over lines and circles, mark their scrambled origins,
take note of undeflected, ice-long trajectories
   and follow them diligently to their natural end
with the gravity and single-mindedness of English Pointers.

   They are like angels, floaters above the scrimmage
or beside it, at once attentive and distracted,
   who always see more than we do, but who,
when you speak of tallies, the campaigns for offensive
   advantage, the imperatives of victory and defeat,

stare blankly and appear to think of higher matters,
    who know how we go wrong, who know the condition
and limits of our movements, our compromised freedoms,
    whispering an advisory word into the big one's ear.
But like us they know nothing of what will happen next.

    And as for their thanks at the final horn,
they are pleased to pass notice, not be deemed
    factors in the outcome. The players file out,
and soon the rink itself, now deserted,
    turns to an empty churchyard under moonlights,

ice spread over stone. Not haunting
    the deserted spaces, they remind us,
as a novelist once wrote, what becomes
    of those who live faithfully
a hidden life and rest in unvisited tombs.

VI Watchmaker God

It's only a game that helps pass the time.
Or that's what the first one dreamed,
who tossed off the whole idea making
figure eights alone over an icy pond.

It goes like this. There is a black hole,
and to start, an entire assembly,
its tension at a peak, is thrown at it.
At a flick, the cranked-up centre wheel

circles clockwise, spins motioning towards
two glancing pinions dropping sideways.
They pivot round the overlapping stud,
and strike straight up at two high-calibre

escape wheels' interlocking checks, now dropped
from their posts, slip wide at the circle top
around the untripped action between them.
The tension shifts. The tail-end spinner

drops in position, takes his feed in turn
and nearing the wind-up flips it on a thread
to the now-turned-in centre wheel driving
both hands at exactly the right time.

The clock stops, and I'll wager the final
outcome that the whole works is carried off
in ways that the first one, now long vanished,
never even dreamed of when he winged it.

VII Netminder

He has a special relationship to emptiness,
   and to all the hollow interior spaces
he keeps others from seeing clearly.
   He isn't talking, but he knows what the absent
gods are for and where they hide. Look
   at how he is never far from the unentered,
forbidden, icy hermit cave at his back,
   and likes to feel it there, fearless of its ghosts.
Masked dancer, shaking his stick, he stalks
   all comers like a shaman, and sees through people.

In a world where we knock about mindlessly
   trying to drive points home for their own sake,
where so much of what we already have
   is spent or frittered away trying to fill up
the thing that cannot ever be filled, not ever,
   it is useful to have an ascetic like this,
cool, level-headed refuser who works
   his shoulders and bulks large on the horizon.

He would have the empty thing stay empty,
   like the ancient goblet under museum glass,
whose guard, unassuming and guileless,
   for the most part standing away, keeps watch
over the void within it and can prove agile
   when a dubious one gets too close.
Perhaps the keeper knows better than most
   how plenitude is not everything it could be.

He knows the size of a man and that no one
    can fill the entrance to his own void entirely,
though that void must by all means be kept
    just as he found it when he came, with whatever
unwakened sasquatch might dwell within,
    the one which, all judgements passed
at the final bell, the keeper can turn from
    without glancing back from the far side,
and leave quietly now to look after itself,
    as though he never needed to be there at all.

VIII Enter, PUCK

Up and down, up and down;
I will lead them up and down:
I am fear'd in field and town;
Goblin, lead them up and down.
            — A Midsummer Night's Dream, III, ii

My cultural horizon was a single line,
    airy, chilled, smoke-coloured ice
three degrees below freezing, the sound
    of clacking sticks like rolled dice,
the hour and the sky always the same.

    Midwinter rinks are their own season,
hard and precise, oval shaped, 200 feet.
    My theatre then was a hockey rink,
a proscenium arch laid horizontal.
    Drama was what you could taste in the air

when the game was tied, just minutes to go,
    and even classical dance no more
than the twirling sashay of our more cocky
    scorers in the neighbourhood. I was fourteen,
had tried poems, but still spent every spare

    minute on the backlot hose-watered rink
firing pucks at two piled railway ties.
    By high school, there were three books I'd read:
Bower on goaltending, a paperback
    of Leaf stats, and a life of Mr. Hockey,

Gordie Howe. But in grade nine English,
    when I looked up, summoned from whatever
makeshift game board's impromptu power play,
    I could sometimes follow almost three
whole sentences of Miss Pearl's trying lecture

    on courtly Shakespearean make-believe.
A month of Tuesdays, the class took up
    the bard's dream of a midsummer night,
something about a king's stately pastimes,
    selves lost and found, and a comprehending

canopy of trees outside the court, where magic,
    with the help of airy sprites, brought folks
to their senses. But never mind. The stage
    she conjured – out of court or wood –
was so unlike our winter's tale of slate-grey

    suburban skies, blunt trees in the snowbanks
like jabbed-in hockey sticks left behind,
    and sad sounds like chalk nicks on a blackboard,
I scarcely bothered to listen. "Mr. Donaldson!"
    Teacher, as always, found me broken loose

on unfettered, imagined breakaways,
    all upriver without a goal in sight.
She looked down with unravelling patience.
    "Welcome back, Mr. Donaldson, so glad
you could join us. Perhaps we could put

those mumblings of yours to better use.
Read for us please from Act II, Scene ii,
  Line 59. Begin with 'Enter, Puck.'
Toby, point out to Jeffery where we are."
  I was showed my place and swallowed hard.

"Enter, Puck." I suppressed a rising snort,
  and heard a snicker like it from the back,
and then two more, then general giggles,
  and almost to preempt them I tried once more,
"Enter, Puck," more gingerly, uncertain,

  to hide an unselfconscious double take.
I had dragged my dream world's assembled
  stage flats and its band of players into class,
where they lingered on like brief chimeras
  to haunt and foil better purposes.

I was no fool. I knew the prankster Peter Puck,
  the cartoon, talking, two-legged rubber disk,
defier of gravity, whose song and dance
  conjured finer aspects of the game
during breaks on *Hockey Night in Canada.*

  But that there should be another like him
to do a master's bidding, to cast vexing
  whammies on all the players he touched,
send them scuttling in a tizzy after him,
  seemed to me more than reasonable.

So read, "I go, I go; look how I go;
    Swifter than arrow from the Tartar's bow."
A master himself of harmless outdoor mischief,
    almost benevolent, selfless, single-minded,
here was a Puck potent as a talisman.

    At last, I thought, a bard who knew what end
of the hockey stick to hold. But Shakespeare?
    I didn't know the game went back that far....
But there it was, no more than a spot,
    pixilated and untrappable,

eluding capture, springing free, tumbling
    and deflecting sportive above the players.
Hobgoblin, you were the black trickster
    that kept me up anights staring at walls,
replaying your shenanigans, your devilish flips,

    with each flitting gesture across the dark
expecting always more dextrous miracles.
    It was like reaching to touch the edges
of an amulet, what for me in time
    became the sole power of conjuring, in a word,

but for now manifestly real and firm
    as the deft weight of India rubber.
It gave me whatever gumption I had lacked
    to recite my last words aloud with confidence,
and read unknowingly for the first time

the line that would spring me open, years on,
as the scot-free boy, chasing in daydreamed
breakaways, up and down, up and down,
the slipped spirit, the bouncing elusive Puck:
"I am that merry wanderer of the night."

Book IV

Knock it down
and lay it on its side.

Cut and split and pile.
Reduce.

Strain cellulose
from lignin,

remove oils
and resins.

Cook wood chips
to slurry,

press pulp
to milled paper.

Form in gatherings,
sew and bind.

Set among others
on the shelf.

An unread book
is like a tree

falling
in an empty forest.

Guesswork

Think of the all too human statistical sacrifice
we'll read of in next Tuesday's paper, zapped
in the tub, or bumped off by a laundry truck,
no part of the weather maker's predictive calculus.

And not even the poets know who will be chosen,
or precisely when, though it will be someone definite
that the bad thing happening will happen to.
Even as you read this, he is somewhere among us,

puzzling over subscription packages for the shows
next year, and what with the spring break
to think about, and the perennials to order
from the April seed catalogue while it is still April.

If only we could find him in the crowd, the poets say,
and take him aside, the one who will leave us next.
But we are blind and live mainly by guesswork.
We go by day into the street among the passersby.

We pull out our hankies and wave them farewell.
We are like lovers left standing alone for a while
on the station platform after the train has departed.
Though there is no train, and the streets are full.

Then and There

There is a certain humiliation in being
found on the streets again this Tuesday morning,
passing out of the local pharmacy with a bag

of purchased toiletries, one licorice,
and a large sign around my neck that says,
"One Who Is Still Living in Time"

written in such large letters and so clearly
that I can't understand why more people
aren't pointing at it. Because in fact,

no one is pointing. No one has thought
to ask me why I've come back,
when I was here last week doing errands

and stepped out of the pharmacy like this,
and it was a Tuesday, the farthest Tuesday
into the future that I thought we had yet

reached at the time. Even then I was
trying to feel that it wasn't wrong to be
there on a weekday morning, bag in hand,

that it was good to breathe the air and notice
that the rain from the night had moved off
leaving a breeze that came up from the lake,

and that it was all right to look ahead,
if I liked, to the week that has now gone by,
without thinking even once about the sign

around my neck, the one that told where
I lived, or of laying it down on the bench
near the empty bus shelter and walking away

from it and coming back some day in the future
to see if it was still there to put on again,
maybe the following Tuesday, if I was free.

Dailygone

a lullaby for Cory

A gold from the sinking sun will rise
up from the treetops into dark skies,

caught in your dreams by the lasting grace
of the day-lit moonlight's sleeping face.

63

Book V

Bound up with echo and allusion,
a book, I have always held,

rarely stands alone,
is more surely upright

leaning on other books,
has ballast and support.

We say "shoulder to shoulder,"
but that isn't it; we rarely stand

that closely ourselves. A book
knows that to touch others

you must fill yourself out,
be all that you are.

Pull down a book anywhere
from the shelf, and the rest

will breathe a long sigh
into the space where it was.

Read in any direction you like,
a row of books has two ends.

Some things you can do with the day when the day is over

You can take it up to the attic in a square box
You can paste it into a scrapbook of days in the empty space marked
  "Yesterday"
You can list it in the classifieds under "Miscellaneous"
You can walk away from it, and if it is still there, you can walk faster
You can take your shoes off and lay them beside it
You can be polite, and say "we should get together again some time"
You can say that you wish things had worked out differently
You can put it at the curb in the recycling bin
You can explain how grieving doesn't help, it is still over
You can ask it what being over is like
You can use it for parts
You can come clean and confess that it wasn't your day
You can become a day whisperer, sit cross-legged at a distance until
  it comes to you
You can lie and say there is no one to blame
You can put it in the mail, addressed to yourself
You can hold it for questioning
You can lie down beside it on a clear night and count the stars
You can try to find one like it among the constellations
You can put off thinking about it until tomorrow
You can tell it the story of the return of the prodigal son
You can make a sculpture of it, starting with a block of wood

Adverbial

Three digs at every moment's perishing
is the storyteller's *then and then and then*...
like shovelfuls of dirt upon the past.
Funereal art, when all is said and done.

Or is there on the line a leaping forth,
a canter which, so near to finishing,
reminds each final word that even *then*
running out of time is the next best thing.

Of Something Seen that He Liked

After the old poet finished his last poem
and read it over quietly to himself,
he folded the sheet once and laid it aside

on the pine desk. He looked forward
to writing another one tomorrow.
The poem is hard to read, folded that way.

But if you peek over his shoulder, you might
make out some of the words that show through
the paper, backwards and inverted.

Things he would be sorry to do without?
There, for instance, you can see
the word "tree" and the word "river."

When a poet leaves a last poem behind,
is it like a squirrel's adding a single nut
to the ample bunch hoarded in the bole

of a maple against the coming winter,
and scampering away? Or is it more like
the confidence of a man who, in a shop,

settles an old account with a last payment,
then turns with a light pocket, whistling?
Or is it the way a child, called by friends,

will leap from a sandbox and leave
one or two toys spread haplessly about,
a red tractor, a shovel for pretend lifting?

The content of this valedictory is anyone's
guess. But look, you are alone now,
and free therefore simply to open out

the folded sheet and read the whole of it,
go looking for that half-glimpsed line that left you
thinking about (how clear it seems now)

the image of a tree clouding water
by a riverbank, backwards and inverted.
And find out for yourself how it goes.

Book VI

The word is like a book:
two hard ends, and between,

small round spaces, verso
and recto, on which to leave

impressions. The whites
of their Tiresian eyes stare blankly.

There is an emptiness
they draw circles around

to keep the word
from being a closed book.

Province House

I propose the adoption of the rainbow as our emblem. By the endless variety of its tints the rainbow will give an excellent idea of the diversity of races, religions, sentiments and interests of the different parts of the Confederation. By its lack of consistence — an image without substance — the rainbow would represent aptly the solidity of our Confederation.

　　　　　　　　　　— Henry Joly, Confederation Debates,
　　　　　　　　　　Monday, February 20, 1865

In the hearts of the delegates who assembled in this room on September 1, 1864, was born the Dominion of Canada. Providence being their guide, they builded better than they knew.

　　　　　　　　　　— Bronze commemorative plaque at
　　　　　　　　　　Province House, Charlottetown, PEI

He read so quietly from a small book,
so mindful of a stillness in the room,
it took a moment to notice he was there,

dimly reflected in the Confederation table's
Pledge-shined oak, glowing with big windows.
The sand-brown brickwork of Province House,

the Island's two-storeyed Palladian fortress,
where tourism and legislature
go joined at the hip along Grafton Street.

Spring morning. The Confederation room
was still unstirred when a cloud ridge pulled off
the horizon. Chilled gaps where the sun rose,

oranging the walls and chairs with a wide .
splash. A tatter of rainbow over the harbour
not so much rising as coming clear.

That's when I saw him seated tableside,
as though he were part of the light he sat in,
and that years of absence had taught him to enjoy

while he could, just by being himself in it.
His hair was like the crest of a sea wave,
its white froth hung over a large forehead,

as though at any point to make a splash.
The Scot's grimace now turned stiff Upper
Canada lip, cleft chin, strong nose for drink,

the rising collar hiding a stilted neck,
an ascot in place of the four-in-hand,
and blue eyes full of a milky distance

in the manner of the old daguerreotypes,
as though the ghost of any man were nothing
but a memory of old photographs.

The leather book he read from was untitled,
as far as I could make out, and seemed filled
with blank pages. He turned them thoughtfully.

"Prime Minister!" I ventured half in jest,
incredulous at my own conjuring,
my voice jarring, like a sudden feedback,

uncalled for and unmannerly, assuming
he'd be impossible to offend as any politician,
who, when spoken to, simply isn't there.

"Right Honourable Sir John! I think of you
as a lingering presence as much
elsewhere in the country as in this room."

He raised his head, looked straight through me,
as though a sound had made him wonder too
about distant ghosts in spite of himself.

"The histories," I tried another tack,
"still speak of you as our founding father,
in a land that famously has no taste

for anything so grand as a Washington
or Napoleon, those fighters for a cause,
heroes or misbegotten madmen throwing off

the ermines of empire to make their mark.
We have a few greyed pictures of old men
raising their towering top hats in the sun,

as though revolution were a picnic.
You there before them, seated on the steps,
small and deliberate as a jockey.

Wily darter among regional thickets,
skirter around inconvenient facts,
you knew how to play ringmaster, rehearse

the premiere and make railroading dreams
appear like circus animals all on show,
put through paces and methodical antics.

Strengthened by spirits carefully distilled,
you came and conquered, convincing the likes
of Tupper and Tilley you wouldn't sell them

up the St. Lawrence River. Good as uninvited,
you and your Frenchman, George-Etienne.
You took his counsel, put some English on it,

your gift of gab, an elixir in two tongues.
You pulled, using the threat of unwelcome Yanks
to spook the room into anxious unison.

You showed us how to elide differences
with metaphoric hyphens, links that, like
the Confederation Bridge, span two sides

always kept at sea. It started in this room,
the plaque insists, with table talk, with words,
not guns, a nation pulled out of a hat,

where the trick is to leave people thinking
they see a rabbit when there isn't one.
That magic still defines us, you must know."

Eyeing the empty tumbler with impatience,
feeling no doubt he'd been tricked himself
into showing up here on false pretenses,

he spoke this time, but without looking up,
as though he'd found a passage in the empty
book that he loved to read aloud from.

I know your kind, teacher—should I say poet?
Which do you prefer? Or when playing cards
do you just follow suit?—who come lurking

in spots like this with your jargoned ideas
of how to make a nation out of words,
perfected in some postmodern classroom.

You like to think metaphor explains it all,
yet something in you knows as well as I
the awkward secret... it explains nothing

at the same time. "But I always thought
that was the point," I countered weakly,
"of impossible unities." *You like*

to be tricky, I can tell, but you can't take
chimeras of that kind to the bank,
or to the capital. In my day, you know,

a pickpocket got jail when he was caught.
You should be more careful what you say.
History in particular, which you like

to mess with like some malleable ghost
out of the past, has a way of showing up
metaphors for what they are: tricks of light,

vanishments, pots of fool's gold at the foot of . . .
well never mind. Just this, an honest man
dreams of hay when he sleeps in a hayloft.

"But faith," I said, "is harder for us now.
In an age of irony and skepticism,
you have to be cryptic to inspire belief.

Your day was different. On the plaque hanging
in the hall, it is written . . . With Providence
your guide, you builded better than you knew!

We have metaphors now instead of gods."
He turned it over. *It was more Provinces
than Providence. But you like this thought,*

*don't you, that while we searched in the dark
we had some idea of a guiding spirit —
like the one you think you see — abiding*

*every time we looked for the right words.
In a way, that idea was our guiding spirit.
Do you understand? It seems to me*

your plaque writer knew his Paradise Lost.
*That final promise, " . . . and Providence their guide,"
was just a crutch, a consolation prize.*

*The trump was Milton's mountain at the end,
the Top of Speculation, where Adam
has his vision of an inhospitable future*

stretched out before them like a landscape.
Faith itself was only an ideal garden
they were banished from, and in place of it

God left Adam with pictures in his mind —
grim events, stations on a pilgrimage,
not to believe in so much as enter into.

He looked out the window toward the street
and seemed to hear a sound in the distance
that he recognized or remembered.

Did you know, that week, the circus was in town?
Think of that. The cries of buskers and clowns,
the ruckus, the devilry and the divination!

There's your metaphor of commonwealth
if you need one. We sat around this table
and tested waters, spied each other out.

Our emergent comings-round were a kind
of serviceable counterfeit. But I felt
that our spirits were echoed in that park,

the great brief tents filling with carnival.
We were caught up in it: acrobats and clowns,
mockers, magicians, jugglers who filled the air,

like us, with more than could be handled.
The perilous breach and the trapeze artists'
timely leap and swing. Blindfolded lunges

for the middle way. Crossed purposes,
where all is a grabbing and a letting go.
Did we see the point and profit of carnival?

Call it metaphor if you like, but to live
by guesses, to suspend belief, not disbelief,
I mean, is faith for the fallen tribes.

Next time you go to the circus — as popular
now as ever, I assume? — keep your eye
on the performers as they step offstage.

Nothing is so real, their faces show,
as fabricated place. On the day
we sailed for home in The Victoria,

we watched them lower the makeshift tents
and drop the flags from their breezy tops,
that they, like us, might set out for new country.

And thus reminded of his slender book,
he picked it up and turned, newly kindled,
the imaginary page, and so went quiet,

lost in his own thought. The light died.
The rainbow was gone, and the dazzled floor
fell to ash under new clouds as the sun rose.

Book VII

Is the last book now in sight,
and is this its homeless elegy,

destined to wander pixilated
on white screens, cut and pasted,

resaveable, its next untyped
character blinking with disbelief?

What the book contained is contained
now in scrolled hieroglyphics.

Still, words come and go, and seem
inclined to lamentation where they fall.

Once more they ask, what are you afraid
of losing? Is it that a book,

a library of books, is at heart a mind
stored where it cannot be lost?

Grief work is never finished,
the mind labouring to put something

less ephemeral in its place.
An elegy is at home in a book.

Acknowledgements

Thanks to the editors of the following journals, who were kind enough to publish earlier versions of poems contained here: *The Fiddlehead, The Malahat Review, The Antigonish Review,* and *The New Quarterly.* Section VIII of "Enter, PUCK" was originally published in *Palilalia* (McGill-Queen's, 2008). Sincere thanks to my editor Anne Compton for her exceptional eye and ear.